TRANSITION

Going From A Good Life To A Great One

By
Crystal Sauls

Dedication

This work is dedicated to all the people who face challenges from childhood. As a child, certain things are unforeseen or unpredicted, and you have no control over them.

Better is the end of a thing than the beginning thereof: and the patient in spirit is better than the proud in spirit.

—Ecclesiastes 7:8 KJV

Acknowledgments

Florence Sauls and William Sauls, support family and friends. I greatly appreciate the words of encouragement, listening ears, and good love and fellowship over the years.

CONTENTS

Introduction

Welcome to Transition!

Thank you! This book represents nearly thirty years of trials, tribulations, ups, and downs of personal experience. Maybe after reading this, you can say the same!

My goal for you is simple: to help you become a better you no matter what you have done or have had done to you. We have new grace and mercy every day. We just have to practice being our best!

Here is what to expect in this book, so you get the most out of it and cure your curiosity.

First: It's reflective. You can think back over your life and pinpoint some things from your childhood that may have caused life to shift you in a certain way into adulthood.

Second: This book is for people with a background in all types of industries, including business, religious organizations, educational systems, and mental health and psychology, to name a few.

Third: This book wasn't intended create guilt about your childhood, teenage years, or adulthood. It's designed to help you start a conversation with yourself, give you a chance to think without the stress that reading this may come with, acknowledge, heal, and move forward . . . *freely.*

Fourth: This book is in English. If you would like to learn more about other languages it is written in, visit www.saulsinternational.com.

This book covers the processes and stages people go through as they shift from one part of their life to the other. This sort of change can be positive or negative, and it can leave you happy, sad, or a mixture of both. The transition can even be serving in the military and going from one branch of service to another. In music, you can change from one key signature to another. Regardless of what type they are, transitions happen all the time. Whether it's a job, business, ministry, music type, a personal desire, age, whatever it is, you are transitioning, and it's a vital part of life. It's a movement.

CHAPTER 1

What Does The Word
Transition Mean?

———— ～⁂～ ————

The word *transition* can be defined as "the process of changing from one condition or state to another." Any transition will have obstacles throughout the process. You just have to be aware enough to recognize the transition, accept it, and see it through. I want to talk about the transition from understanding myself, what's going on with me, what has been going on throughout the years and what I'm destined to do and how I'm going to get there.

Behavior

So first of all, with transitions, I had to realize that I had to evaluate my personal life to include my interactions with people and vice versa. I had to transition from being used by people in general into standing up for myself. This means that I had to take a stand for things that were right, not wrong. This was big for me because making the conscious decision to take a stand was different but necessary. Also, a lot of these actions that I went along with in life were not right. In all honesty, you can't just go along with any and everything, and you can't think that you're going to continue to get by with things for long. Being humans first and having a sin nature, you are liable to say and do things that are not right throughout the course of your life. However, you don't know the consequences of what your actions are going to be while you're doing these things. This is how you begin to transition into negativity without even being conscious of it.

Observations

So one of the issues I faced most of my life was having men mentally, verbally, and sexually tamper with me, and women verbally and emotionally tamper with me from a very young age into my adult life. When this happens to a young person, some of those traumas and dramas follow you into adulthood, which doesn't make for a positive transition. You can actually take on some of those ways if you keep allowing it to be a close part of your inner circle.

Because of the character, morals, and makeup of some women that I have been around, I can say that all interactions, gestures, and comments were not always bad but weren't always favorable. If your female friends are laughing at things that are serious or don't warrant a laugh, belittling your talent, skills, or goals or being snappy and sharp in the tongue, you just have to realize that the friend you thought you had has now transitioned into someone you know, and all you can do is be "friendly." It's sad to watch this with groups of women. You really have to get to know the spirit of a person before you say they are a true sister or a friend.

I can say that I haven't done everything right, and I may have had an attitude here and there, but I didn't stay in that funk all the time! My mom would even tell me about my little mouth and attitude from time to time, saying, "Maybe Crissy is on her cycle!" Or, if we were out at an event and I was helping with the setup, mom would say that I was being snappy. These things were true, but I didn't mean any harm, and it truly was not my norm. In my situation, I could have been bothered about something at the time, trying to rush to get things done, or it could have been anything. In other women, it could be other relationships causing women to act in such a manner. Either way, if I was in a funk, God always brought me out, whether it was three days or three months! That's why it's important not to stay in a negative state of being throughout the entire course of your life. That's a fast way to transition into sickness, mental stress, and other issues.

Dreams Seemingly Shattered

Most women dream about being married and having kids. Women don't dream about being in relationships that turn into disasters. As far as the men go, they are considered to be the head of the household or family, and women and children should respect them as such. When a man doesn't operate in his role of being the head the way God intended him to be, the entire structure of the family gets out of whack. When I was a child, men would say things to me and touch me in places they shouldn't. I just thought I had to go along with these things. As time went on, I started confronting some of these things.

As I got older, of course I wanted to have a boyfriend and get married like anyone else would, but the relationship didn't turn into marriage. It seems that everything was a continuation from my childhood with a little more fire put into the furnace! You know when you get a certain age, you try things and go along with certain things. The thought never comes to your mind that you are getting yourself into a world of trouble by following your heart or going along with things. I was in relationships with the hopes of getting married. So as a woman, I found myself being in cycles of being in dead-end relationships and having my spirit, mind, and body degraded by someone who never thought enough of God and would never think well enough of me to do right, make things work, and be together the right way. I used to think that every good thing that was said to me was true and real. Later, I started getting good at paying attention to the things that were said that were not so pleasant. I had to start putting it all together and noticed that these actions and things said would play in my mind on repeat. This is how you start feeling sad, unhappy, or unsatisfied. It played on my emotions, mood, and positive intentions. I was even blamed for certain things that were not my fault. And a side note, if I ever led anyone on to make them feel that way, I always apologized and asked God for forgiveness. At this point, I was feeling used, but at the same time, it was recurring, so I noticed that this was some negative attraction or hellish assignment that had been sent my way. I realized that God has always spoken to men, and men are very intellectual, so I needed to get good at knowing what spirit was using a man or woman when they interacted with me! Needless to say, I had to recognize when God was warning me or showing me something too! I wasn't exempt. Therefore, I had to get to the root of all of this and noticed that I had to regain my spiritual power, faith, and ambitions to the highest degree and start shifting into a better personal life.

Adult Interactions with Children

When you're a child, you have no control of what adults do to you, and for the most part, you don't want to say anything because you feel like an adult won't listen to you and you'll get in trouble if you do say something. You think the person you tell will say something like: "Well, you lying on them anyway, so, you know, we don't want to hear it." What I realized was that same promiscuous lustful spirit that had been bothering me through other people when I was young transitioned into my teenage years. In your teenage years you face puberty. You're a pure, untampered with person. I started out this way, as I wasn't trying to be promiscuous. However, I was around people who were trying to pressure me. I didn't want to give up my virginity when certain people tried to get me to. Later, I tried different things, and when you do this and do that, you don't think it is a big deal—or at least it wasn't to me. At those ages, nothing was a big deal. You just did stuff! But others I was around had obviously already started with all of that.

So I was put in positions where I thought I had to take this or go along with sexual content or verbiage. This was my experience with men who would corner me in different places. This began that kind of life for me off and on, but it was never a desire of mine from the beginning or on a regular basis. It was never an appetite, and then you get into your older teenage to early twenties years, and you want to be in a relationship, and then you're still with somebody who's lustful and never satisfied, and you feel like you are never enough anyway. It just gets into this pattern of somebody using you now because you are in this so-called official boyfriend/girlfriend status. And this is what boyfriends and girlfriends do, but the end result for me was never marriage. These guys never intended to marry me, and even if they, did they wanted me to marry them on top of the drama they were already doing, so it was like I would have to go along with it. If I did, I wouldn't be successful at relationships at all. I saw that these were more failed relationships that had some of the same off communication while still interacting with the same lustful spirit. Therefore, this type of behavior followed me from childhood into adulthood while I didn't know what it was.

CHAPTER 2

People & Their Giftings

When you are born, whatever you are destined to be is already a part of your makeup. As you go through life, you morph into what you are supposed to be. In addition to being born to be great, you also develop talents and gifts along the way. Have you ever noticed that you like certain things you liked as a kid or have certain goals for your adulthood as you did when you were a kid? You grow up saying that you want to be a doctor, firefighter, singer, or what have you. If you haven't noticed, you will have major obstacles, losses, wins, and victories as you work toward your goals. You may be gifted in certain areas, but you have not been mentored in those areas to gain experience and knowledge, so you go through life aimlessly sometimes. Either way, this is all part of your transition, and you will start noticing what your talents and gifts are, and then you have to put in the work to develop them.

There are many gifts that one can have. You can have a gift to play musical instruments, write, sew, cook, see things before they happen, judge the character of a person, be a mathematician, encourage people, etc. Since we are focusing on the topic of transitions, we will focus on gifts that you have that are spiritual. For example, there are many people that can spot a liar a mile away, detect great things that will happen for you, warn you of tragedies that may happen if you don't shift your ways and environment, or help where needed.

I grew up in a Pentecostal, apostolic, deliverance-like church. As I got older, I helped out in music departments at Baptist churches. I later went back to a Pentecostal, apostolic deliverance church in my early twenties. Throughout the years, I served in various capacities in ministry. The teachings in the Pentecostal and apostolic ministries were always that of heaven or hell, live holy to make it into heaven, and do good to your brother or sister. After doing a lot, going along with a lot of things, and seeing a lot, I realized that you have to be a pure vessel to serve in ministry just as Mary was the pure vessel that carried Jesus in her womb. My course for being pure had already been nullified as a young girl, so I had to go through different transitions to be pure as I got older. Side note: Jesus didn't say that Mary was saved and filled with the Holy Spirit. She was a pure vessel that had never been touched by a man. That's what qualified her to do the work. We are qualified to give birth to greatness once we are pure, and we take the time to consciously stay pure in every aspect of our lives. Transitioning into being pure as an adult is spiritual, mental, emotional, and physical. That is not easy, but for some, it's doable. Don't let the negativity from your past be the current setback of your daily life. You have a bright future ahead, and you have to move toward it.

Your Transition to Serve

Does anyone talk about being pure to serve in the religious arenas? Nobody really digs into the importance of being a pure, clean vessel to serve on an auxiliary, on a board, or in a department. In my adult years, I was taught that you need to be pure to serve in ministry, which means you need to be pure of heart, mind, spirit, soul, body, attitude, and mood so God can get the glory out of your vessel that He's using. Along my journey, I found that people are serving in ministry, and they're not delivered/free from negative things that have happened to them from their childhood and adult years. Now they are adults and are serving in churches and places of worship. Some of these people have titles and are leaders over groups of people. They work with different departments and are hurting from time to time, and it shows through their mannerisms. In these cases, sometimes the anger, rage, or emotionalism flares up or lust will come across into the environment surrounding the people being served.

If you are an adult serving in a religious organization or any department working with young people, you should seek counsel if you know you have a history of being angry, being inappropriate with them, or doing anything that is not conducive or positive. Young people are vulnerable and still develop behaviors and mannerisms based on their environment. It's better to develop young people with all positivity. They are like sponges—they absorb things! Let them absorb all the positivity they can! As they get older, the world will be enough for them to experience.

Witchcraft & Your Spirit

As you transition into learning more about the good deeds you are supposed to do and the pure life you are supposed to live, you start a journey of searching yourself. As you search yourself, or for a better word, *monitor* yourself, you will see that others around you may or may not be on the same journey. I started realizing this as I was repenting every day, trying to be a better person and keep myself on the path to greatness. I also realized that I was around some people who were and were not repenting and trying to be a better person. Some things are just harder for some than for others. So there is a scripture in the King James Version of the Bible that says something like this: when I would do good, evil was present.

I had a cousin that always used to say: "Evil is following me." No matter what your beliefs are, what religious organization you are a member of, or your level of spirituality, you will face adversity as you journey through life. The goal is to recognize who you are, what you are doing, and who you are around. You are either going to be in the presence of witchcraft or purity in your home, at work, at church, and anywhere you go to spend your time. Just monitor your actions, words, and deeds to make sure you are not inadvertently speaking curses over people, practicing the art of witchcraft, and opening yourself up to having a manipulating spirit. Most people don't know this is going on with them, so they continue to act the same way around certain people, which now transitions into a negative lifestyle and negative actions that they are certainly not aware of but others are. If you continue this negative behavior, you will start to shift your environment from bad to worse, and others around you will feel this heaviness or darkness that has become your new life. This is not a good transition, but you will definitely transition into inviting negative spirits into your presence, and now your supposed transition to a better life will have transitioned you to a negative spirit with the addition of principalities and wickedness.

CHAPTER 3

The Battle – Wicked Transitions In Places Of Worship

Have you ever had a battle inside of your mind that stemmed out to your actions? I mean a battle of good versus evil? In places of worship, good is supposed to be happening. Take for instance the Charleston 9. There were nine people enjoying a night of fellowship at Emanuel African Methodist Episcopal Church in Charleston, South Carolina. During the service, a man came and opened fire on those who were there. I believe this was a wicked transition that took place among people who were doing a good deed.

Some people in religious organizations have gifts to see certain things and discern certain things, and some people don't. It was just natural for people in religious settings to continue to do ministry over top of all of the ungodliness. But what happens is when you are actually called to do something, you have an anointing to do something in ministry, God wants you to be a pure vessel and not a tainted vessel. If you are overtaken by bad actions, deeds, or thoughts, you don't have to stay that way. That's what repentance and deliverance are for. So what has happened to me is that I didn't know that all the years of being tampered with, even the years of trying different things, would result in soul ties, promiscuity, and having that same trail of demonic spirits following me. I dated people who were friends with people who were into witchcraft. Of course, I didn't know it at the time I was dating them. I found all of this out after the witchy activity had started happening and was in full effect.

Throughout all of this, I even thought to myself: that's not the life I wanted. I wasn't out here prostituting. I wasn't voluntarily acting crazy on a regular basis like this is who I am. No. I wanted to be married.

I didn't know the witchcraft was going to flare! This happened because I was dipping and diving into ungodly territory with other people and God was not a part of those activities! I wasn't practicing witchcraft, but if God is not in certain things, the enemy is!

I wanted to have some structure, but I didn't want to be used, nor did I want to use others. Those negative spirits will always attack those who really want to serve and work wholeheartedly, especially depending on the anointing God has for you.

So as I was trying to serve in ministry, I noticed that I wasn't as pure, and I wasn't as comfortable in trying to serve all the time. It is so different trying to serve when you are upset, tired, tainted, etc. versus not being these ways. Of course, I wasn't like this all the time, but when I was, I could tell the difference. I would look at others in places of worship and wonder if they felt the same way, if they weren't as pure or comfortable trying to serve.

I didn't understand why I was feeling like that until God revealed to me exactly what was going on with me. I had a history of promiscuity that started as a child who didn't know how it would affect me in the long run. In all actuality, deep on the inside, I really didn't want to be that way. I didn't want this type of behavior to be my lifestyle just because I was in a relationship with a man. But I am glad I eventually noticed that's the spirit that had been trailing me. So when you are in positions, you know you have to be aware of your own battle and the other battles coming your way. You can't be in position and be blind at the same time.

The Relationships Didn't Work

Most girls have their eyes on some cute young man in their teenage years and vice versa. It's just common to like someone when you are young, but it's not common to have so many unsuccessful relationships with bad incidences to happen. No one in their right mind would think they are going to encounter unimaginable situations with someone they desire to spend their life with. And we all know that most relationships have ups and downs. Both parties are responsible for their own actions. I can admit to not being up to par if I have habitually said or done something that was not right or something that may have bothered him. However, I did not deserve some of the things that happened to me, nor did I feel good about the negative things I have done. I had a guilty conscious, and I didn't feel like myself, so I had to do things to make myself feel better. For better words, I felt convicted! I noticed that the men were really not free. Some were still holding on to past relationships by keeping in touch with their exes, some were angry at times, and some just had their own battle that no one could help them fight. They probably never asked God for help. If you date someone like this, you never have a chance at the relationship because the person has never transitioned from whatever has been holding them back. They technically are not available. The communication for some things was there, but not good enough for any changes to take place long term. To feel better, I just had to leave the relationship. *Freedom*!

My relationships wouldn't work even though I would be committed and exclusively his. And when I came to the understanding that something unusual was happening, I could mentally do something about it. Me desiring to be the only pure one in the relationship was still not going to work because it takes the two people in the relationship to commit. Your purity isn't just benefiting you when you are in a relationship with a human being. It's for any type of work you do. You don't want someone cooking your food or servicing your vehicle if they are not well.

Now it took a while to understand what was going on in these raggedy, wild relationships. I mean years. Honestly, spiritual leaders and others would warn me about some of the things (not all) as they were happening or after they happened. I would even be warned in my dreams. I just had to stop being fearful and face the adversity that was in front of me.

CHAPTER 4

Working With Young People

––––––––– ⟡ –––––––––

Currently, there is a shift in how young people worship or plan to attend religious events. Back in the day, older people used to go to church and were grateful for making it through life's transitions. They had a better appreciation for God and all that He made happen. Young people today are more vocal and opinionated when it comes to what type of work, they will accept, friendships, and spending time at spiritual events. Young people also have a place in houses of worship, and most good leaders will do things to attract young people. However, you have to keep in mind that young people need guidance and mentoring.

In houses of worship, everybody just can't be serving and doing ministry out of religion. It should include some spirituality. Young people go through lots of changes, and they normally look up to adults, so adults should be as pure as possible if they are serving young people.

If you are currently serving and you are tainted while doing administrative work, you have tainted worship, or you struggle to make simple decisions, continue to work on your issues so you can serve better. It's OK if young people have issues, but as an adult, work with them simply because you know how teenagers and young adults can be and they know how you were. Young people will eventually get better as they grow and come into the knowledge of what they are supposed to be doing in ministry.

Always take a step back and look at your actions.

What Do You See in Yourself?

When you answer the question, "What do you see in yourself?" you think of all of the good things. Right? Well, we should all tell the truth and say that we have knowingly done some wrong in our lives. We all have the capacity to do good and evil. We often tell people that we see the good that we do and we have improved over the years. So the reality is, we have ways that are a part of our DNA, or we picked up habits along life's journey, whether good or bad. We have been around good influences and bad influences at an early age. It's exciting when people talk about how good we behave or acts of kindness, but it's not so good when people notice a negative transition in our behavior, character, appearance, etc.

I saw the good and the bad in myself over the course of two decades. What I didn't like was the fact that negative things were happening to me that probably didn't need to happen. After evaluating everything that was happening to me, I realized that some things could shift for the better if I did something about it, and some things, I had to go through to take a stand for myself and what was right. I also received warnings, prayers, the preached Word, and spiritual resets throughout the years, but some things you go through are for you to acknowledge and do something about it. After thinking back on my childhood and young adult years, I picked out the root of one of the main issues I faced on a regular basis. The root of what happened to me is that there was a lustful appetite in men that was following me throughout the years. Once you continue engaging with this appetite (knowingly or unknowingly), you open yourself up to several types of promiscuous behaviors and spirits which are now part of your trail. I unknowingly kept encountering the same thing with different people. It didn't matter if the man was in church or not. Actually, some of those in ministry were not free from those ways, and some actually didn't think there was a problem with how they were. This goes back to my question: What do you see in yourself?

I still saw the good in me, but I felt bad over time because of the negative interactions. Being that I grew up in good churches, I wanted to be like the good ladies I saw. There is a cost that is associated with being a good person and keeping up that reputation. Now I transitioned from what I saw to what I felt. I felt like the bad appetite and spirit inside of people was trying to destroy me, destroy my spirit, attitude, and dreams. These types of people could care less about the work of God in themselves or me. They didn't really care about serving and being pure at the same time. We all had our own convictions and dealt with them in our own way. Any major negativity could have been avoided with better communication, openness, and honesty. Without these components, you are working with these factors: steal, break down, and kill. Everyone I was around getting positive insights and words of encouragement spoken to them. They were obviously getting the message, but they didn't care about a lot of it like I did.

Transitioning from Different Types of Spirits

There are always these different spirits and energies around you. Along with that, you are around anger, pride, hurt, and other things that are not so good. At some point, you've soul tied into these things and the spirits that don't want to let you go without knowing it. Even though you want to let it go and you may not be so involved, those spirits will still try to take you over if you don't do something about it. Opening yourself up to evil spirits is no good for anyone. It can be more work than a little bit to be delivered from. I noticed these things happening to me from time to time, but God always made a way of escape. This was an important transition in my life, and it's something always to be watchful of.

Be mindful of the company you keep and who you entertain. I also had to be mindful of my own spirit so I wouldn't negatively impact somebody else. After getting prayer and having dreams about certain things, I had to be more proactive by praying for myself and cutting back on the places I went. Atmosphere and environment are majors' part of your existence as well.

CHAPTER 5

Prepping For Marriage

———— ❧ ————

I wanted to be married and be with my husband, and we enjoy each other. I didn't want to have all this other negative stuff going on and try to be in a relationship at the same time. Neither did I want to be with someone who had a secret life. Some people have an appetite for lots of things going on at one time, but that's too much to juggle. As far as marriage, I was around people who were in relationships, and they were doing what most all couples do: fight, argue, go out on dates, buy each other stuff, have sex, go to family functions, etc. These couples were women and men who were coworkers, church members, family, and friends. A lot of them got married. I didn't. There are young and old people who didn't get married, and they have their own reasons. As long as I was in the dead-end conversations and relationships, I would never be properly prepared for marriage. I had to get to the root of this.

The root cause and the root issue was seeing that I spent too much time in relationships that were not headed toward marriage the way God intended. After reflecting on my goals for the relationship and their goals for the relationship, I concluded that these people were dating me with the intent to destroy the positive works I wanted to do, to tear up my mind, spirit, body, and soul.

As time went by, I learned that some of the people I encountered were full-blooded witches working witchcraft. They were warlocks that surrounded themselves with positive and negative people whether they knew it or not. And most of them didn't even know this was what they were around until it was told to them. At this point, you have to really pay attention to who you choose to be friends with and who you choose to date. In all reality, it's not just you and the person you are with. It's who they are around as well. Sometimes you have to detach yourself from what may appear to be harmless but is not. Needless to say, I made sure I cut off anybody else that wasn't going to add to me.

When you are preparing for marriage, there is some general house cleaning you should do to ensure a fresh start. Some things you can do are as follows: make sure you are over the last person you were with, stop spending time with them at their leisure, and stop saying terms of endearment to them and keeping the door of communication open to them. As you know, it's hard to stop everything all at once, so a lot of people are still in communication with people with whom they were in relationships. Some will move on with other people and add this new endeavor to their life when they are not completely over the past relationships. We all have fallen victim to this. Remember that we are trying to prepare for marriage, so it's time to start fresh! Being that the past relationships didn't work, you've added all these spirits, and a lot of times, you're not on a spiritual level to fight those demons that are coming at you through somebody else. Spiritually, you must clean out your house! Keep yourself clean and ready for marriage because the enemy is waiting and lurking to visit you with plans to come to steal, kill, and destroy your purity.

So I had to realize in my transition from being pure and being set apart that you can't go along with the men who are trying to be abusive, jealous, prideful, or lustful or just want to go against your wishes. You must be strong. You can't go along with the woman who's cheering you on to be lustful and have no conscience about being out of the will of God. There were a few people I was around who wanted to be set apart and holy and just really sold out to the Lord and talked about how they wanted to be set apart or about some of their personal struggles. We all have a struggle. I always felt like I was by myself to some degree. But the issue is, I was never told by a prophet in detail that I had been battling a lot of spirits and these other spirits inside of men would try to overtake me. I was told that men just wanted to be with me to use me for my body. It's just one of those situations where you must be honest with yourself and what's been going on, talk to God about it, and do something about it while you are single and prepping for marriage.

CHAPTER 6

Understanding Your Transition

————— ～✦～ —————

Some things we encounter, whether positive or negative, are generational (in your bloodline), cultural, or geographical. Some aunts, uncles, grandparents, or cousins will tell you about things that have happened in the family way back in the day. Sometimes the detail that is told to you will help you understand why you are going through certain things. That's where the saying, "There is nothing new under the sun," comes from.

I grew up around women who were strong in their conviction to stay with their husband or long-term partner no matter how bad things got. I always looked at the positive and didn't think much of the negative over the years. I always thought that God was forgiving, and I should be the same. It came to a point where I noticed that forgiveness given from me didn't make a difference simply because the men were going to do their own thing whether it was done around me or not. Honestly, some things just went over my head. Now you see why I had to transition into being more aware of what was said to me and done to me by males and females. After I would share different things that happened in the relationships with people, they would say things like, "Cry's, you know you're being used," "She said what to you?" "You dated who?" "What were you thinking?" "You did what?" etc. The spiritual leaders would say things like: "That guy needs to be delivered," "You know if you keep sinning, you'll go to hell," "You need to keep yourself," "You can't keep your anointing and keep dealing with that person," "Be aware of your surroundings," etc. I understood all of that, but everybody around me, or for better words, a good majority of people I was around, were doing the same things.

So I was always around those specific types of spirits. We all are! When I came to realize that I could handle my interactions differently and fight to be a better person during these transitions. Even when I would do better, there were those who would still try to try me. I call it flare-ups. When I would speak up for myself and tell them what I had to tell them, let them know that I was not available for certain activities, they would get all mad and upset, even snappy. That's on them! That's deliverance for me! I couldn't keep accepting a life that I never wanted, so I had to do the best I could with discerning what would show up.

In the past two or three years, I would reflect on my actions and other things that were not good. I would reflect and say: "Look at this craziness!" However, it wasn't until the coronavirus pandemic and being quarantined that I really found out the root of what was going on. We couldn't be around a lot of people, and life as we knew it had changed. This was my time to reset!

I used to help out with music departments at different churches, and some people would downplay me in the position I had or encourage me in the position. Regardless of the positivity or negativity in any position I had, I was still facing the penalties of sin whether God sent me to help somewhere, or man gave me the position. So whether I was singing or playing a musical instrument or serving in administration, sin is sin. Doing your due diligence to be pure, have a good attitude, and have positive interactions was a necessity when doing a spiritual service based on how I grew up. If I didn't keep these statutes, when I went to do my godly act, it wouldn't be as spiritual and pure, as I was tainted by doing ungodly acts. From time to time, I was thinking to myself, "Most everybody else is doing the same thing. Why does it seem like I am the only one getting penalized and penalized so badly?" I mean, it looked like the favor of God was leaving me left and right, front and back. I missed out on millions of dollars in contracts and missed a possible opportunity to have a decent husband all because I was tied up liking somebody who just wanted to use me, but I couldn't see the end at the beginning. I eventually felt like I'd been used and was not doing God any good service either. But the fact is, I have a separate gifting than others and vice versa. Regardless of anyone's gift, we are all held accountable for our interactions, spirituality, and attitude. This was never prophesied to me or told to me that way. I didn't really grasp it until I sincerely asked God and He let me know what was really going on.

So at this point, I'm transitioning into being a pure woman and fighting off every demonic force that comes at me. I am praying to understand those spirits that will try to pop up and hinder me, no matter who it is in. They transfer so they can get into anybody at any time. I don't care if they are family members, next-door neighbors, or strangers. Regardless of anyone else, I just want to be better. Not bitter! You have to know how to discern and fight in the Spirit. So your transition has to be from being passive and smiling all the time or super excited to being more quiet, watchful, discerning, and prayerful.

I thank God for the transition into understanding what's going on with me and who these spirits were coming through. I also had to understand that all the people I was around might not have appreciated any position I had—even if it was helping them. I served in ministry and business, but I felt that I was not anointed enough to do anything. I understand that sometimes it can be a lonely walk when serving or transitions happen. So now we are transitioning from being used to fighting more in the Spirit and having more spiritual armor and ammunition. And now that we have this ammunition, we are in a better place. I am in a better place to serve purely, to hear from God purely, not to have everybody and everything in my ear. Acknowledging this was a blessed setup for me to better myself during the pandemic.

CHAPTER 7

Transition During The Coronavirus Pandemic

———— ✦ ————

During the onset of the coronavirus pandemic, you couldn't rely on going to church as usual. Most churches were closed, and they transitioned to being virtual. You weren't responsible for anything other than what was in your house because you couldn't go out and do everything. No more big conferences. No more big travel. None of these big gatherings were going on anymore. So you had the time to get with God, pray, fast, and really build your spiritual awareness, your anointing, and all the spiritual things. I believe this had to happen so you could sustain during the pandemic and when the pandemic was over. At the end of the day, He gave you an anointing to work, have a family, and spread the good news. The anointing is not just to hold it for yourself and say, "I am anointed by

God." If you get too arrogant and cocky, He does reserve the right to take it away from you.

I transitioned into spending time with God more and did not deal a lot with who I was around before and who would try to creep up and come up during the pandemic. I had to deal with things in a certain way (spiritually and naturally).

I had spent time on a spiritual and mental seesaw, so now I just wanted to get good at spending time with God, so I could get ready for my next sets of assignments. I transitioned first within myself to understand what I was doing wrong, outside of the will of God. Then I had to transition into fighting in the Spirit and putting those spirits in their place, so they would leave me alone. Later, I had to transition my thinking in the sense of not letting other people's negative ways, mouths, and actions overtake me. Remember, not only was I dealing with men, but also I was dealing with women with their different ways and spirits. Things that were done and said were not always godly or positive, so I found myself fighting for my peace and contentment while feeling like I was being sifted, like I spiritual leeches were draining the spirituality out of me. I would turn on my favorite songs on YouTube or do something exciting to counteract the negativity taking place.

In the first year of the pandemic, God anointed me and said he would heal me. I didn't even know He was anointing me, but several prophets called me and said that God was anointing me and healing me while I was at home. I set myself apart, reading and praying, doing spiritual things, being obedient, fighting off the enemy.

Now when I go to lay my hands on doing what God has placed for me to do, he sets an anointing over it. How do you know it's anointed? Because it's blessed and there is a positive impact. You can feel the positivity. You have your health, you have finances coming, and when you go to sing and play, if you're a musician in the church, there's an anointing on what you're doing. If you go speak somewhere, there's an anointing on you speaking. Now, the things that you say are going to impact somebody positively. This must become your way of life. I've got to be groomed that way. I was told that my grandfather, who was a pastor, had a mantle, and there are some people in our family who have to carry on the mantle. Well, what is the mantle? I was a little girl when he passed, and I didn't see all the great things he did in the Spirit, but I was told he had an anointing to cast out demons. People would come in drunk and leave out sober. They had these different spirits when they would come in, and they would leave without those spirits. They left all healed and delivered, and whatever that process looked like, he was an anointed vessel to carry it through. But I had to realize during the pandemic that I was being attacked by demons and demonic forces. That's why my stuff seemed to be a lot heavier than that of the other women I was around. That means I have an anointing to fight off these demons and not let them keep overtaking me.

CHAPTER 8

Greatness

———————

So now we're moving forward in our transition to greatness. It was great to transition to greater anointing and greater works. It isn't for me to flaunt, but it's in appreciation to God so He can get the glory. I don't ever need to be famous. I don't need to be well-known. I don't have to be appreciated or thanked all the time, but I have to get God's work done because I can't live a life where I'm beat up by allowing negativity to intrude my space. I also had to realize that I couldn't allow myself to be an enemy as well. When you are not in the will of God and you don't want to keep being out of the will of God, you have to work really hard at monitoring your actions. We are powerful, and it's important to know what to say and how you react to things.

A Better You

My life is different than those of others around me, and I don't have to spend my life explaining this. No one should live a life where they always have to be explaining themselves. I just want to thank God for the various things He showed me about myself and others around me and how I can transition into greatness. So no matter what position you're in, you need to serve purely, have a pure heart, and have a conscious mind. If there are people doing things that are not of God and they're around you and you feel like you can't say anything, you've got to pray about it and transition yourself from dealing with them.

Then you have to make a life out of transitioning into greatness and purity so you can get your blessings and your rewards on Earth. Your life is not supposed to be hellish all the time. You're not supposed to be warring and fighting these same things all your life. If you are, you are in a vicious cycle of things, and you have to get a handle on what's going on. You have to get to the root of it, and the benefit of living in the pandemic was that you didn't have to be around all that same stuff anymore because you were only responsible for your household. You shouldn't have stayed in any vicious cycles.

If you were not an essential worker, you didn't have to go and deal with those spirits on the job. You didn't have to go deal with a full congregation of people, because the churches couldn't be full even if you were battling with people at church. You didn't have to worry about big conferences and going to see this and that person you had to work with. Your battle with things before the pandemic was one thing. During the pandemic, the focus was about getting yourself delivered and being in a better spirit and position for when it was time to get back into the church building and to the job and into the schools. It was time to reset!

Pay attention to your life, your cycles, your history, your route, and your family. Understand your path to greatness and understand your path to transitioning into having a better life. It starts with you first as an individual, then what's around you, and then what you're going to do moving forward and how are you going to move. The spiritual gifts, the fruit of the spirit, and the gifts of the spirit are what I call God's *principles* or *code of ethics*. If you follow the principles, you can have a better life. This walk of life is not a walk that everybody understands or cares about. You're not going to have a lot of friends. You're not going to have a lot of family who want to be close to you, because their tests and trials are different than yours, and that's okay. Embrace your transition and the things you have to do. God is always in your transitions, whether you acknowledge it or not. If you are with God and you are into God, you will notice that He was with you whether He sent an angel or a person to say something to you. Even if you didn't notice this before or acknowledge it, you have grace and mercy every day, and you should be more aware of His interactions with you and do all that you can to listen and obey. You just don't make rash decisions on your own as if God is not there.

As you start getting better at listening to God, don't start judging people and pointing fingers because you don't feel like they are listening to God. You have to remember that we all face challenges and handle them in different ways. Sometimes the challenges are rough, and you feel as though those spirits around you come to destroy the work that you are supposed to do. You also have to keep in mind that you go through different things at different times than others. People around you may not notice this. When you think back on your life, you notice all that has happened and those spirits and how they dealt with you. Now, you can discern these spirits better as you journey in life. You may be able to help someone now that you have gotten better at some things.

God's blessings don't add any sorrow. If the people you were dealing with added sorrow to your life, they were coming to destroy the positive works that you set out to do and they didn't even know that they were vessels being used by the enemy. They were geographically set up at different locations and times in your life to test you, from birth to date. These people were at work, at home, school or sitting in someone's religious organization etc. You probably didn't know how to react to all of this as it was happening. Moving forward, you will do yourself some justice by being able to discern what's going on around you.

You don't know what spirits are following you. You don't know what spirits are around you, especially if you haven't been taught about the types of spirits. If you have never experienced deliverance in a spiritual setting, you're not going to know these things. After weeks, months and years of trying to be a better person, you realized that you faced difficulties and uncertainties that you would have never imagined. Because of this, your eyes are open! Moving forward, remember that you are better at discerning what's going on around you and what's going on within you. Now, you can produce what it takes to be a better you!

CHAPTER 9

Being Aware

————— ✻ —————

If you're not around any prophets or you don't have a fivefold ministry around you, you're not going to know a lot of these things. So this stuff seems like it's the norm. Look at *Forensic Files*, *Rescue 911*, the ID channel, or *Dateline*. The occurrences on these shows look as if this is just life and these things just happen. No, it's all spiritual. I've sat in services where people were warned about things that would happen to them if they were around the wrong crowd, kept going the same way or doing certain things.

Reflecting to the TV shows that I mentioned earlier, when disaster happens to these people, I would often think to myself that they might not have been around a prophet or received any other warning. They might not have been a member of any church denomination. They might not have been warned. Maybe they were warned and were disobedient. But either way, everything is always spiritual, so you have to know how to war in the spirit. That doesn't mean laughing all the time, buddying up with negativity, or ignoring what's in front of you. It means being more aware of your surroundings.

It's a great thing to be more aware, especially if you are not used to paying attention to certain things. Honestly, this is one way to build your spirit man. This is how you build your legacy. This is how you build your life in Christ. You have to do spiritual things and get spiritual armor so you can succeed in life and move forward. So, I challenge you, examine yourself, purify yourself, your body, your spirit, and your soul. Eat well. Exercise! Repent and transition into greatness.

You don't have to take somebody talking to you nasty, to the point where it's getting on your nerves and stressing you out! This is one-way sicknesses start brewing in your body. You are not designed to feel like you have to take all of this turmoil. Turmoil and stress are not your portions. Victory and freedom are your portions!

Positive vs. Negative Transitions

If your transition brings you joy, be excited! If it has you feeling a little sad now but will bring you joy later, gauge your levels of sadness and happiness so you can have balance. Though you may be uncomfortable, understand that your transition process is different, and you don't want to come off like you're being negative when you talk about the changes you had to make. You don't want to come off appearing like you were the victim all the time. You transitioned because you felt that it was necessary.

We have seen, even on January 6 on Capitol Hill, all the drama that will take place when people who are like-minded get together and cause planned chaos. No one knew that Capitol Hill would be stormed and raided and that there would be shootings and outrage resulting in multiple deaths. The political climate was that of verifying the presidential candidate. Instead, we all watched the world go through all this turmoil. You don't want to be a part of that number of going from turmoil into drama. If you're a person that's wholesome, good spirited, positive, and have spent your years getting better, you don't want to think anything tragic could happen to you or others around you. Everybody came from being something that was unseemly, but you've spent your latter years getting better. You don't want to get into the habit of being in agreement with things from the top down.

Your personal transition involves one individual: you. Now what happened at Capitol Hill was the transition from one president to the next and just verifying candidates from state to state, and that transition is never peaceful. It is always drama filled. This time, however, it involved all these emotions and feelings and really just turned our country into something it has never been. So if the world is going to be in disarray from the top down and allow these things to happen, or if people get together and make our world look divided like this, we sure can't have a life of craziness at any point.

Presidential transitions and personal transitions should be peaceful if possible. The process of making decisions to transition from an office of an organization, a job, or a relationship is not always peaceful and easy, but it is necessary, so you have to do the necessary planning and implementation. Now you have to deal with the aftermath of your decision, which is kind of more your mental state, physical state, emotional state, spiritual state, and those types of things. Keep in mind that you have to do things that are best for you, and sometimes that's also best for the people around you.

Your transition has to start within you first. Somebody can tell you you're going to go through different changes, but at the end of the day, you have to process all that and determine if you are going to really be in transition. Ask yourself: "Is it necessary? How's it going to affect me? What's it going to affect? When? Who? What? Where? When? How? Why?" You know, are you going to start determining your transition?

Explaining Your Transition

Be careful with who you feel like you need to answer to when it comes to your transitions. The powers that be are those you probably need to answer to, and you need to think that through really well. Your decision doesn't have to involve a lot of people. Your transition may involve a lot of people, or it may not. It just depends on your situation.

CHAPTER 10

It's Your Time

It's time for greatness, and it's time for great transitions. All you have to do is just watch as well as pray, watch your dreams and right visions, and watch others around you so you know how to pivot and how to transition when it's time, whatever that looks like. That's your call of duty.

You feel different things at different times, and it's not planned, and you really don't know how you're going to react. Understanding the undertaking that your physical body is going through and mental state is one thing, but your emotional state is just as important. There are sometimes when you're excited, happy, and relieved, and there are sometimes when you're sad. We all experience a little crying here and there. At the same time, our emotional state has been like a roller coaster—the crying and then thinking about different responses to a comment that you would have made and how someone would have responded or how somebody did respond that wasn't so nice, leaving you with that feeling of hurt and sadness. These are just normal processes. You're not physically going to be around the same people anymore. You either have to be alone for a while at the beginning or just get comfortable with doing new things by yourself. It's just something that you take day by day. Especially if it's fresh. You've got different challenges, feelings and emotions, and thoughts every day. You may not like the process, but it's necessary. And so you have to go to these stages of what I call deliverance to honestly be free, and you want to be free to move forward and do the things you are called to do. You should always be moving toward your destiny.

As you move toward your destiny, get rid of situations that involve drama, craziness, ruthlessness, and all these unseemly, ungodly things. These are things that are the opposite of the gifts and fruits of the spirit that are in

Galatians 5:22-23. If you are still facing issues and your issues seem to be something that you can't shake, counseling may help. If there are some close friends or family that are helpful and instrumental in this process of you reaching your destiny, connect with them. If you have a great mom, dad, uncle, etc., it's good to be around them as well. Being in their presence can lift your spirit. They will usually say something encouraging, and that's important.

It's good when people can be supportive. Good family and friends are a good support system when you're going through transitions. They are probably supportive because they went through what you went through. Maybe they don't understand all that you are going through, but they want to be there for you. Good friends are not biased, and they don't try to bash you for your decisions or try to take your side or anybody else's side. They are just available because it's just the right thing to do. It just means so much to have a good team of people that are available for you as you transition, as close-knit, supportive environment. You could be content with a set of friends who is just emotionally there for you. You don't have to dump on them or anything, but just having their support is good. Nobody's being drama-filled. Nobody's tale-bearing, gossiping, or saying all this stuff.

In conclusion, let your life's journey be a lesson to catapult you into greatness day after day, month after month, and year after year. You are someone special, and you are destined for greatness whether you feel like it or not. We are all in processes and transitions, and we must learn to make the best of it. Do the best that you can do and go for the gold as you transition!

About The Author

Crystal Sauls fell in love with idea of writing books years ago and continues to love the art of it. Today she is pursuing her dream of being a published writer and business owner in between the multitudinous demands of adult life. She pulls her strength, motivation, and courage from God with expectations of greatness and newfound mercy each day. When she has a free moment, she enjoys reading, learning about marketing, music, foreign languages, cooking and time with God. Crystal can be found on Facebook, Instagram @crissyssound and on LinkedIn.